THE ELEMENTS

Zinc

Leon Gray

Marshall Cavendish
Benchmark
New York

Marshall Cavendish Benchmark
99 White Plains Road
Tarrytown, New York 10591

www.marshallcavendish.us

© Marshall Cavendish Corporation, 2006

Library of Congress Cataloging-in-Publication Data

Gray, Leon, 1974–
Zinc / Leon Gray.
p.   cm. — (Elements)
Includes index.
ISBN 0-7614-1922-5
1. Zinc—Juvenile literature. 2. Zinc alloys—Juvenile literature.
I. Title. II. Series: Elements (Marshall Cavendish Benchmark)
QD181.Z6G73 2006
546'.661—dc22

2005042163

1 6 5 4 3 2

Printed in China

Picture credits
Front cover: Boliden
Back cover: Atlantic Metals & Alloys

American Galvanizers Association: 1, 5, 18t, 18b
ARS: Stephen Ausmus 27, Jack Dykinga 24, Keith Weller 25, 26
Atlantic Metals & Alloys: 4
Boliden: 14, 15
Stan Celestian: 11cl, 11bl, 11br
Corbis: Lester V. Bergman 7, Christine Osborne 23
International Zinc Association: 19
Mary Evans Picture Library: 10
NASA: Marvin Smith/GRC 22
Photos.com: 20, 21
Science & Society Picture Library: Science Museum 8
Science Photo Library: Andrew Lambert Photography 16, 30, TH Foto-Werbung 12, Charles D. Winter 3, 6
University of Pennsylvania Library: Edgar Fahs Smith Collection 9

Series created by The Brown Reference Group plc.
Designed by Sarah Williams
www.brownreference.com

Contents

What is zinc?

Pure zinc is a hard, brittle, blue-white metal that belongs to a group of elements known as the transition metals. People have used zinc for more than two thousand years in the form of brass. Brass is an alloy (metal mixture) of copper and zinc. However at the time people did not know that brass contained two metals.

Zinc and its compounds have many important applications today. The main use of zinc is for galvanization. This is a process that applies a thin coating of zinc to the surfaces of objects made from steel. Galvanizing stops the steel from rusting. Car parts, ship hulls, and many everyday metal items, such as bolts, are made with galvanized steel. Zinc is also used to purify water and in large batteries, such as those used to power electric vehicles.

The zinc atom

Everything in the universe consists of tiny particles called atoms. Atoms are the building blocks of all the elements. They

Pure zinc is shiny but its surface quickly dulls as it reacts with oxygen in the air.

These steel poles are being dipped into liquid zinc during galvanization. The zinc coating will stop the steel beneath from rusting.

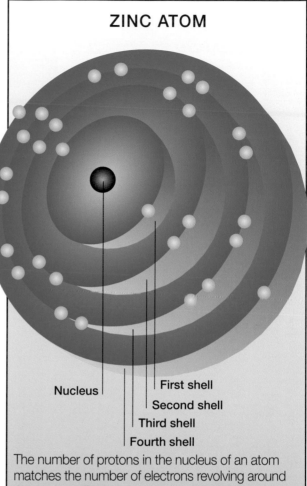

ZINC ATOM

Nucleus | First shell
Second shell
Third shell
Fourth shell

The number of protons in the nucleus of an atom matches the number of electrons revolving around the nucleus. Each zinc atom has 30 protons in the nucleus and 30 electrons. The electrons revolve around the nucleus in 4 layers, or shells. There are 2 electrons in the inner shell, 8 in the second shell, 18 in the third shell, and 2 in the outer, shell.

are very small—too small even to be seen with a microscope. The period at the end of this sentence would cover about 250 billion atoms.

Atoms are made up of even smaller particles called protons, neutrons, and electrons. The protons and neutrons cluster together in the dense nucleus at the center of each atom. The electrons revolve around the nucleus in a series of layers, or shells.

The number of protons is represented by the atomic number. The atomic number of zinc is 30, so there are 30 protons in each zinc atom. The number of protons and electrons in an atom is always the same, so every zinc atom has 30 electrons revolving around the nucleus. Protons have

a positive charge, but electrons have a negative charge. The positive and negative charges of these particles are equal and cancel each other out. Therefore an atom has no overall charge at all—it is neutral.

Neutrons also have no charge. Zinc has different versions of its atoms, called isotopes. These contain different numbers of neutrons. Most of the zinc isotopes are

Zinc is a reactive metal and often forms compounds with other elements. This test tube is filled with acid. The zinc and acid react to form a salt (metal compound) and bubbles of hydrogen gas.

radioactive, which means they break apart into other elements. However, there are five stable zinc isotopes.

The chemistry of zinc

The electrons in a zinc atom occupy four shells. The first three electron shells are full, but the fourth shell has just two electrons and there is room for more.

The number of outer electrons determines how an atom reacts. A zinc atom has just two outer electrons, and these are easily taken away by atoms of another element. Zinc reacts most often with elements that have one or two spaces in their outer electron shell. These spaces would be filled by zinc's outer electrons. After losing electrons, the zinc atom has a positive charge and is called an ion.

Zinc compounds

Compounds are made when atoms of two or more elements bond together. The atoms combine to form structures called molecules. Zinc is reactive and forms many different compounds. Useful zinc compounds include zinc oxide (ZnO). This white substance is also called Chinese white. It is used in paints. Zinc sulfate ($ZnSO_4$) is used as a fertilizer.

Zinc is essential for life, too. All living things, from plants to people, need zinc to grow normally. The metal is found in more than 300 enzymes. Enzymes are large molecules that control life processes.

Special characteristics

The bar of zinc at the top is bright and shiny, but powdered metal is much darker because it does not reflect light in the same way.

Pure zinc is very shiny, but the metal reacts quickly with oxygen and moisture in air. This reaction covers the surface of the metal with a thin film of zinc oxide (ZnO). The zinc compound makes the metal look a dull gray.

Compared to other metals, zinc has a low melting point. It turns into a liquid at 788 °F (420 °C). If it is heated above this temperature, the zinc then begins to boil and turn into a gas at 1665 °F (907 °C).

Below 212 °F (100 °C) pure zinc shatters easily. However, between 212 and 302 °F (150 °C), the metal becomes more malleable, which means it can be easily bent. At these temperatures, zinc also becomes ductile, which means it can be drawn into fine wires and threads.

ZINC FACTS

- Chemical symbol: Zn
- Atomic number: 30
- Atomic mass number: 65.39 (average)
  (The number of protons plus neutrons)
- Melting point: 788°F (420°C)
- Boiling point: 1665°F (907°C)
- Density: 7.133 g/cm^3 (7.133 times the density of water).
- Isotopes: Five natural isotopes and sixteen artificial isotopes

Zinc as a metal

Like most other metals, solid zinc is made up of many crystals that are too small to see with the naked eye. Each crystal consists of many zinc atoms packed together in a six-sided pattern. The crystals form sheets of atoms that can slide past one another without breaking apart. This makes it possible to bend the metal.

Inside the crystal, the zinc atoms lose their outer electrons. These electrons float freely throughout the crystal structure, allowing the metal to conduct both heat and electricity easily.

The history of zinc

Long before zinc was discovered as an element, people were using zinc ores to make brass. The earliest brass objects date back more than two thousand years to ancient Greece and Rome. Metal-workers made brass from copper and a zinc ore called calamine. An ore is a natural rock or mineral that contains a lot of metal. Calamine contains zinc silicate [$Zn_4(Si_2O_7)$].

The ore was heated with charcoal (a carbon-rich fuel made by heating wood) in a large pot called a crucible. Copper granules were layered at the top of the crucible. The zinc in the ore turned into vapor and rose to the top of the crucible. Then it mixed with the copper above, which was beginning to melt. This formed brass alloy, which was then melted completely so it could be poured into molds.

Zinc in Asia

The first people to identify zinc as a single metal were Indian metalworkers in the fourteenth century. They made zinc by heating calamine with wool in a crucible. The zinc vapor flowed into a condenser (a tube cooled by water) under the crucible

A small brass coin from 330 B.C.E. showing the head of Alexander the Great, a Greek emperor.

until it became solid. By the sixteenth century, zinc production had moved from India to China. The Chinese made vast quantities of zinc and sold it abroad.

Zinc in Europe

One of the first Europeans to describe zinc was German mineralogist and scholar Georg Bauer (1494–1555). He was better known by his Latin name Agricola. He wrote a book called *De Re Metallica*, which was about mining and metalworking.

In the book Agricola described an unknown white metal, now known to be zinc. Agricola saw the metal when it was produced by accident when lead and silver ores were being purified at a smelter in the Harz Mountains in central Germany. However, Agricola did not realize that what he had seen was a new element.

Agricola, the German mineral expert, described a great number of naturally occurring substances, including zinc and its ores.

By the seventeenth century, Arab, Dutch, and Portuguese traders were importing zinc from China. By this time, many European scientists knew about zinc and were looking for ways of making the metal themselves.

One of the first was English scientist William Champion (1709-1789), who first produced pure zinc in 1740 by heating calamine with charcoal to make zinc vapor. The vapor was collected in a cone-shaped cylinder called a retort. The vapor escaped through a hole in the bottom of the retort and was then condensed into solid metal in a water-cooled chamber. By 1743, Champion had built a large zinc smelter in Bristol, England. This was the first zinc smelter in Europe. Zinc continued to be produced in Bristol until 2003.

In 1746, German chemist Andreas Sigismund Marggraf (1709–1782) developed a method of zinc production that was similar to Champion's. By describing his method in great detail, Marggraf established the basic theory of zinc production. For this reason, he is often credited with the discovery of zinc. Zinc takes its name from the German word *Zinke*, which means "point." This refers to the shape of the metal crystals as they condense after heating.

Soon afterward Swedish chemists Anton von Swab (1703–1768) and Axel Fredrik Cronstedt (1722–1765) used local zinc ores to make brass. This meant that calamine no longer had to be imported from Asia.

Improving production

In 1798, German scientist Johann Ruberg (1751–1807) improved the efficiency of zinc smelting by using several horizontal retorts around each crucible. This allowed the metal to be made continuously and saved on fuel used by the smelter.

At first, calamine was the main ore used by brass and zinc producers. However, soon they turned to smithsonite (zinc

DISCOVERERS

ANDREAS SIGISMUND MARGGRAF

Born in Berlin, Prussia (now the capital of Germany), on March 3, 1709, Andreas Sigismund Marggraf was a leading chemist. He was the first person to distinguish between the compounds alumina (aluminum oxide; Al_2O_3), magnesia (magnesium oxide; MgO), and lime (calcium oxide; CaO). Marggraf also developed a new and improved method for producing phosphorus. Perhaps his most important discovery came in 1747—a year after he first isolated zinc from calamine. Marggraf extracted sugar from sugar beet. This laid the foundations for the modern European sugar industry. Later in 1754, Marggraf was appointed director of the chemistry laboratory at the Berlin Academy of Sciences. He retired in 1760 and died in Berlin on August 7, 1782.

carbonate; $ZnCO_3$) and later sphalerite (zinc sulfide; ZnS). Sphalerite was roasted to convert it into zinc oxide. The oxide was then added to the crucible.

Zinc in the United States

By 1810, Belgium was the world's largest zinc producer. However, the United States began making zinc in 1850 using retorts. By 1907, the United States was producing 230,000 tons (207,500 tonnes) of zinc a year. That was more than 30 percent of the world's total, making the United States the world's leading zinc producer. Today Australia makes the most zinc.

This zinc ore mine in Poland was employing men, women, and children during the 1860s.

Where zinc is found

Zinc exists almost everywhere in the environment—in air, in water, and in the soil. However, the metal makes up just a tiny fraction of Earth's crust—on average about 2 to 3 ounces (56 to 84 grams) in every ton of rock.

Astral origins

Scientists think that all the zinc on Earth formed inside giant stars. The energy inside these giant stars is so great that lighter elements, such as hydrogen and helium, fuse to create the atoms of heavier elements, including zinc. When there are no more small atoms left to fuse into larger ones, the stars explode, forming bright supernovas. The explosions blast the new elements out into space.

The explosion created a huge cloud of atoms, containing many heavy elements, including zinc. Eventually the cloud formed into the Sun, Earth, and the other planets.

Zinc minerals

Zinc never occurs as a pure metal in nature. It is always found combined with other elements in the form of minerals—compounds locked away inside rocks. The most important zinc minerals are sphalerite (zinc sulfide; ZnS) and smithsonite (zinc carbonate; $ZnCO_3$). Other minerals include zincite (zinc oxide; ZnO), franklinite (a mixture of oxides of zinc and iron), and marmatite (a mixture of zinc and iron sulfide).

Zinc minerals are found in many rocks all over the world. In a few places these minerals are more common and form deposits of ore. These deposits contain enough zinc to make it worth mining. Then the ore is purified, or refined, into pure zinc metal.

Zinc minerals have a range of crystal structures and colors. Smithsonite (top left) is orange, willemite (left) is white, while zincite (above) makes pink crystals.

From ore to metal

Sphalerite is the most widely used zinc ore. It contains zinc sulfide, as well as small amounts of other metals, such as indium and cadmium. Most sphalerite is found in Australia and North America.

Zinc ores are found in most parts of the world, but nearly half of the world's total supply comes from mines in Australia and the Americas.

The mining method used to recover the ore depends on the properties of the mineral. Oxide ores, such as zincite, are usually found near the surface, so these deposits are collected by digging a huge hole, or pit, in the ground.

Sulfide ores are buried deeper beneath Earth's surface. Sphalerite is a sulfide and it is the most common zinc ore. Because it is found so deep down, complex underground mining techniques are needed to bring the deposits to the surface. Deep shafts are dug down to the ore, which is then dug out forming large caverns.

DID YOU KNOW?

RECYCLING ZINC

About a third of the world's zinc supply comes from recycled zinc. Sources of zinc include car parts, brass fixtures—such as door handles— and household appliances and electronics made from galvanized steel. Zinc is also recovered from factory waste. This includes scraps of metal cut off during manufacturing and the leftovers from refining and galvanizing. Zinc can be recycled many times without weakening the metal.

Preparing the ore

Only a tiny amount of zinc sulfide is present in the rocks taken from the mine. Before pure zinc metal can be made from it, the unwanted rock must be removed. This is done by flotation separation. In this process, crushing machines grind the ore into chunks. The chunks are mixed with water and crushed again, forming a thin oatmeal-like slurry of fine powder.

Air is then blown through the slurry inside a water tank. The zinc sulfide in the slurry clings to the air bubbles as they travel up to the surface. This forms a zinc-rich froth, which is skimmed off.

The froth is dried out and roasted in air. This causes the zinc sulfide to react with oxygen gas in the air. The oxygen

ATOMS AT WORK

The first stage of refining zinc sulfide ore is to heat it in air. Air contains oxygen, which reacts with the ore.

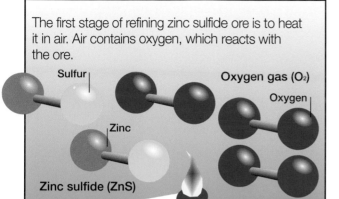

Sulfur

Oxygen gas (O₂)

Oxygen

Zinc

Zinc sulfide (ZnS)

The bonds between the zinc and the sulfur atoms break apart. The zinc atoms forms new bonds with oxygen atoms and make granules of zinc oxide.

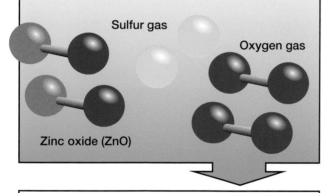

Sulfur gas

Oxygen gas

Zinc oxide (ZnO)

The sulfur atoms react with other oxygen atoms. They form sulfur dioxide gas. (The sulfur dioxide is used later to produce sulfuric acid.)

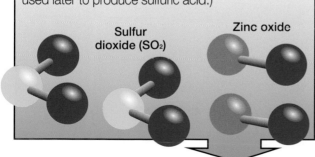

Sulfur dioxide (SO₂)

Zinc oxide

The reaction that takes place can be written like this:

2ZnS + 3O₂ → 2ZnO + 2SO₂

replaces the sulfur in the ore. This converts the sphalerite into white zinc oxide crystals (ZnO). The sulfur from the sphalerite combines with more oxygen to make sulfur dioxide gas (SO_2).

Refining by electrolysis

In one method of zinc production, the sulfur dioxide is used to make sulfuric acid (H_2SO_4). This acid reacts with the zinc oxide to produce zinc sulfate ($ZnSO_4$). The sulfate is dissolved in water. As it dissolves, the compound splits into zinc (Zn^{2+}) and sulfate (SO_4^{2-}) ions. The zinc ion has given two electrons to the sulfate ion, so both have an electrical charge.

The charged ions can carry electricity through the water, and this is a way of separating out pure zinc. This process is called electrolysis, which means "splitting with electricity."

Electrolysis involves running an electric current through the zinc sulfate solution. (A solution is a liquid containing a dissolved compound.) The current runs between two electrodes. The positive electrode is made of lead and silver. The negative electrode is a sheet of aluminum.

Electricity makes the positively charged zinc ions move through the solution toward the negative electrode. There, the zinc ions collect electrons and form a thin layer of pure zinc metal on the aluminum sheet. The sheet is removed every few days and melted down to separate the pure zinc from the aluminum. The aluminum is remade into sheets and used again.

The zinc-lead blast furnace

Another method of zinc production involves heating zinc oxide with coke inside a blast furnace. (Coke is a carbon-rich fuel made by roasting coal). The zinc oxide and coke are placed at the top of the furnace, and hot air is blown through holes, called tuyeres, at the base of the furnace.

A giant excavator is used to dig out zinc ore in a cavern. The cavern was dug completely by miners.

The reaction that takes place in the furnace is an example of an oxidation-reduction reaction. Zinc atoms from the zinc oxide lose their oxygen atoms and form pure zinc metal. Chemists call the process of losing oxygen reduction. At the same time, the carbon atoms in the coke bond with oxygen atoms and form carbon monoxide gas (CO) and carbon dioxide (CO_2) gas. Chemists describe this part of the reaction as oxidation.

Zinc has a low boiling point, and it boils in the heat of the furnace. The zinc vapor is collected in a lead-splash condenser. Inside this chamber, rotating paddles shower droplets of melted lead

Pure zinc is molded into large bars, or ingots. Each ingot weighs about 2 tons (1.9 tonnes).

into the zinc vapor. The vapor mixes up with the liquid lead. As the two metals cool down into solids, the lighter zinc atoms form a layer of pure liquid zinc on top of the heavier lead atoms. This upper layer is then drained off, and the lead is melted down and used again.

Distillation refining

Blast furnaces produce zinc that contains small amounts of other metals, such as lead and iron. The impurities in the zinc can be removed by a process called distillation. Distillation is used to separate things with different melting and boiling points. The impure zinc is heated inside a tall column. Zinc has a lower boiling point than the impurities in it, and zinc atoms are the first

ones to turn into a vapor. The other metals stay as solids or liquids at the bottom of the column. The zinc vapor cools as it rises up the column and can be collected as almost completely pure zinc.

DID YOU KNOW?

ZINC PRODUCERS

The leading producers of zinc ores are

Australia	1,675,000 tons (1,520,000 tonnes)
China	1,650,000 tons (1,500,000 tonnes)
Peru	1,270,000 tons (1,150,000 tonnes)
Canada	1,100,000 tons (1,000,000 tonnes)
United States	816,000 tons (740,000 tonnes)
Mexico	524,000 tons (475,000 tonnes)
Other countries	2,760,000 tons (2,500,000 tonnes)

How zinc reacts

A strip of zinc is dipped in a blue solution of copper sulfate. The zinc replaces the copper to make zinc sulfate. This reaction also produces pure copper. This brown metal collects at the bottom of the tube.

The chemistry of zinc is controlled by the behavior of its electrons. A zinc atom has four electron shells. The first three shells are full, but the outer shell contains only two electrons.

Losing electrons

To be most stable, atoms need full outer electron shells. Atoms will react with each other to achieve this by either gaining or losing their outer electrons. During chemical reactions, zinc atoms release the two outer electrons in their fourth shell. This makes the third shell, which is full, the outer one, and the atom becomes very stable.

When an atom loses or gains electrons during a chemical reaction, it becomes an ion. All ions are charged. This is because they have either more or fewer electrons than protons, and the charges of these particles do not balance. An atom that loses electrons becomes a positive ion. Gaining electrons produces negative ions. When a zinc atom loses its two outer electrons it becomes a zinc ion with a charge of +2 (Zn^{2+}).

Ionic bonds

During chemical reactions, ions are formed when one atom gives its outer electrons to another atom. (This second atom uses these electrons to fill up its outer shell.) Reactions like this produce both positive and negative ions.

Opposite charges attract each other, and the ions cling together to make compounds. This is called ionic bonding. All zinc compounds are ionic. For example, zinc carbonate ($ZnCO_3$) is made up of zinc ions (Zn^{2+}) and carbonate ions (CO_3^{2-}). (Carbonate ions include carbon and oxygen atoms.) Chemists call zinc compounds (and most other ionic compounds) salts.

Solid zinc salts are a mesh of ions, bonded together to make crystals. When a salt crystal is dropped in water, it dissolves, forming a solution. As it dissolves the ions separate and mix with the water.

Reactivity

Zinc is more reactive than most metals, such as iron and copper. This is because it is more likely to form ions.

When pure zinc is added to a solution of another metal salt, a displacement reaction takes place. During a reaction like this, the zinc atoms form ions that push out, or displace, the ions of the other metal. The zinc releases electrons that are picked up by the other metal ions, which then turn back into atoms.

For example, if pure zinc is added to a test tube of copper sulfate ($CuSO_4$) solution, the zinc disappears and lumps of solid copper gather at the bottom of the tube. The zinc has displaced the copper to form a solution of zinc sulfate ($ZnSO_4$).

Metal-acid reactions

Zinc also reacts with acids to form a salt and hydrogen gas (H_2). For example, when zinc reacts with hydrochloric acid (HCl) it forms zinc chloride ($ZnCl_2$) and hydrogen. This reaction works in the same way as when zinc displaces a metal. The electrons from the zinc turn hydrogen ions into atoms.

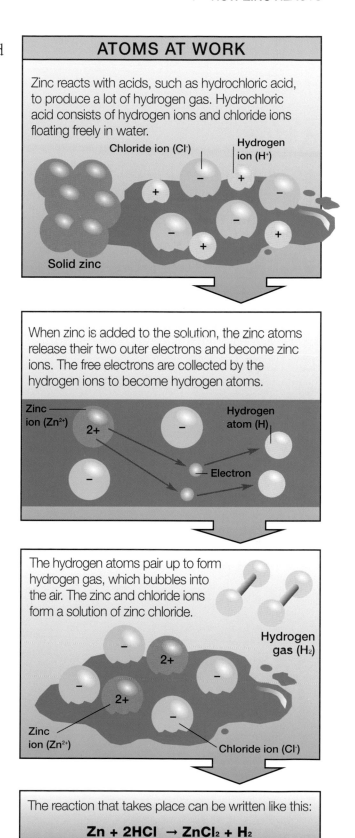

ATOMS AT WORK

Zinc reacts with acids, such as hydrochloric acid, to produce a lot of hydrogen gas. Hydrochloric acid consists of hydrogen ions and chloride ions floating freely in water.

Chloride ion (Cl⁻)   Hydrogen ion (H⁺)

Solid zinc

When zinc is added to the solution, the zinc atoms release their two outer electrons and become zinc ions. The free electrons are collected by the hydrogen ions to become hydrogen atoms.

Zinc ion (Zn^{2+})   Hydrogen atom (H)

Electron

The hydrogen atoms pair up to form hydrogen gas, which bubbles into the air. The zinc and chloride ions form a solution of zinc chloride.

Hydrogen gas (H_2)

Zinc ion (Zn^{2+})   Chloride ion (Cl⁻)

The reaction that takes place can be written like this:

$$Zn + 2HCl \rightarrow ZnCl_2 + H_2$$

Galvanizing

When steel is exposed to oxygen and moisture in the air, a chemical reaction takes place. This reaction is called corrosion, and it involves iron atoms in the steel reacting with oxygen to make rust. Corrosion weakens the steel, and the cost of replacing rusty objects costs billions of dollars a year.

A thin coating of zinc is used to protect steel from rust. This is called galvanization. The zinc forms a barrier between the iron in the steel and the air. Even if some of the zinc is scratched off, the surrounding zinc still protects the steel underneath. Because zinc is more reactive than iron, the zinc reacts with the air first. This fills the scratch with zinc oxide and seals the steel inside.

These metal poles are being galvanized by being dipped into hot liquid zinc.

As they react, the zinc atoms give up their outer electrons. As a result tiny electric currents flow through galvanized metals. The word *galvanized* comes from Italian scientist Luigi Galvani (1737–1798) who discovered electric currents.

Liquid zinc

The main method of galvanizing involves dipping steel into a bath of melted zinc. In some cases long steel sheets are passed through the zinc bath. Such sheets are used to make cars and building roofs.

When an object is too large to dip into a bath of zinc, melted zinc is sprayed on using a heated gun. The hulls of ships are

These steel bolts have been galvanized. They will be used in damp places, such as outdoors, where uncoated bolts would rust and weaken quickly.

galvanized in this way. Steel rusts very quickly in salty conditions, so the hulls must be well protected.

Blocks of zinc are often bolted to other underwater objects, such as the legs of oil platforms. The zinc reacts with the salty water in place of the other metals present.

Using electricity

Objects can also be galvanized using electrolysis. An electric current runs between a block of zinc and a steel item. This current runs between the metals through a solution of zinc.

The electricity makes the zinc atoms give up their electrons and become zinc ions. These dissolve in the solution and are carried by the electric current to the steel, where they form a thin coating.

These buildings in Dresden, Germany, have roofs made from galvanized steel.

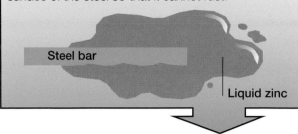

ATOMS AT WORK

Steel is galvanized by dipping it in liquid zinc. This coats the steel with a protective layer of zinc. The zinc keeps air and moisture away from the surface of the steel so that it cannot rust.

Steel bar

Liquid zinc

If the coating is scratched, the iron (Fe) in the steel reacts with the oxygen (O) in the air, producing rust (FeO). As it reacts with oxygen, the iron loses two electrons to make Fe^{2+} ions. Zinc atoms give up the two outer electrons and become ions. The electrons flow through the bar to the iron ions in the rust. The electrons turn these ions back into iron atoms.

Scratch in zinc layer | Rust (FeO)

Electron

Galvanized steel

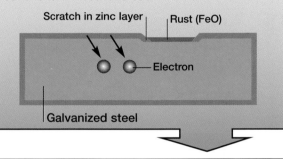

Zinc ions replace the iron ions in the rust. This turns the rust into zinc oxide. The zinc oxide seals the scratched area and so the coating continues to protect the steel underneath.

Zinc oxide

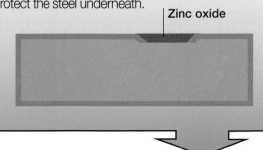

The reaction that takes place can be written like this:

Zn + FeO → ZnO + Fe

Zinc alloys

An alloy is a mixture of metals. The metal that makes up most of the alloy is called the parent metal. Other metals are added to the parent metal to make it stronger or more resistant to heat or corrosion.

The most important zinc alloy is brass. The parent metal of brass is copper. The amount of zinc in brass ranges from 10 to 40 percent. Different amounts of zinc in the brass change the properties of the alloy.

Decorative brasses

The Romans discovered how to make brass about two thousand years ago. At that time people did not know that zinc was a metal itself and they did not know how to make pure zinc. Metalworkers must have learned how to make brass by chance.

One of the first uses of brass was to make coins. Today, many small, low-value coins are made from zinc alloys.

Over the centuries, craftsmen have used brass to make decorations such as statues and jewelry. By the beginning of the twentieth century, brass was being commonly used to make corrosion-free metalwork, such as door knobs, faucets, and other household fittings.

Today brass is being replaced by more modern materials, such as plastic and steel. Although it is still used, brass objects are much less common. However, many wind instruments, such as trumpets, are still made from brass. Brass instruments contain about 35 percent zinc, making the alloy light, strong, and easy to shape.

This lock is made from brass. The zinc alloy will stay shiny for a long time.

Other types of brass

Brass is not just used to make shiny objects. For example, cartridge brass contains about 30 percent zinc. This alloy is unusual because it bends more easily when it is cold and hardens when it gets hot. Cartridge brass is used make bullet cases. When the bullet is fired from a gun, the heat created does not soften the brass case, like it would with other alloys.

Naval brass contains about 40 percent zinc and a small amount of tin. The tin and zinc stop the copper in the brass from corroding in seawater. Manganese bronze, is a strong alloy with small amounts of iron, manganese, and aluminum. This alloy is used in pumps and valves.

Other zinc alloys

Zinc is used as an ingredient in many other alloys, including nickel silver and solder. Nickel silver was used a lot in the

Zinc is one of the ingredients in many metal coins, especially smaller coins, such as pennies, that have only a low value.

nineteenth century to make inexpensive silver-colored objects. Solder is an alloy that melts easily and is used to stick pieces of metal together.

An alloy of zinc, copper, and titanium is used to cover large buildings. An alloy called Prestal, which is 78 percent zinc and 22 percent aluminum, is as strong as steel but bends easily like a plastic. It can be molded into any shape. Another alloy of zinc mixed with aluminum and magnesium is very strong and light. It is used to make airplanes.

Zinc in technology

The fabric of the spacesuits used by the crew of the space shuttle is coated with zinc oxide. This coating absorbs the strong ultraviolet radiation found in space and protects the astronaut inside.

Most of the world's zinc is used to make brass or to galvanize steel. However, pure zinc and its compounds also have many other important uses in science and technology.

Die castings

Many everyday machines, such as cars, computers, and water heaters have zinc components. These zinc components are made by die casting. In this process melted zinc is injected into molds at high pressure. The zinc then cools into a hard solid. One of the most common die-cast objects to contain zinc are zippers.

Zinc oxide

Zinc oxide (ZnO_2), is perhaps the most useful zinc compound. Also known as Chinese white, powdered zinc oxide is a brilliant white. It has been used as a pigment (colored substance) for many thousands of years. Zinc oxide is still used to make paints and inks.

Another important use of zinc oxide is as an additive to the rubber used to make automobile tires. Zinc oxide can withstand high temperatures, and it prevents the tires from breaking apart when they get hot.

As well as absorbing heat, zinc oxide also acts as a barrier to ultraviolet light. Ultraviolet light is invisible light produced by the Sun. It causes harmful sunburn and makes skin become tanned. Zinc oxide creams are used to protect the skin.

DID YOU KNOW?

SHIELDING SPACECRAFT

Scientists at the U.S. National Aeronautics and Space Administration (NASA) developed a zinc oxide-based coating to protect its spacecraft, such as the space shuttles. The coating can withstand the high temperatures produced when flying back into the atmosphere and the high levels of ultraviolet light found in space.

Zinc glows

Things that glow in the dark contain substances called phosphors. When light shines on a phosphor, some of it is absorbed and released later on. In the dark, the phosphor glows as this light is slowly given out.

Zinc sulfide (ZnS) is an important phosphor. It is used as a coating on watch dials, so they can be read in the dark. It is also used to line the inside of fluorescent lights and television screens.

Water purifier

Zinc's reactivity is used to clean dangerous impurities, such as iron and chlorine, out of water. Dirty water is passed through granules made of zinc and copper. The zinc atoms lose electrons and become ions. These ions dissolve and displace other metals in the water. The free electrons are picked up by other dissolved impurities, which become harmless or turn into a solid. The solids produced by these reactions are filtered out leaving very clean water.

High-powered batteries

Zinc-air batteries are a new type of power source used in cell phones, laptop computers and electric vehicles. The battery produces electricity when electrons flow from a zinc plate inside the battery to oxygen atoms in air trapped inside. This produces zinc oxide, which must be removed regularly.

This lifeguard is using zinc oxide paste to protect his skin from strong sunlight.

Zinc in crops

All plants need a supply of zinc to grow properly, and crops—plants grown for food—are no exception. Even in soils that have plenty of water and other minerals and are free of damaging pests, crops will not grow healthily without zinc.

Plants only need a small amount of zinc to be healthy. The zinc is used to make enzymes. Enzymes are complex compounds that control all of a plant's life processes. The enzymes containing zinc control the plant's growth and the way it makes food and seeds. Zinc is also important for fighting off diseases.

A plant needs zinc from the very beginning of its life. The first root growing out of the seed absorbs minerals from the soil, which are needed for the rest of the plant to grow. If the root cannot get enough zinc, the new plant cannot grow as quickly as it needs to in the early days and it will never recover.

Zinc deficiency

Most crops are affected by a lack of zinc, but grains, such as corn and wheat, are particularly at risk. When these crops do

These farming experts are checking that a field of wheat is growing as well as possible. Wheat and most other crops need a supply of zinc to grow.

Too much zinc in the soil can also stop plants from growing. This alpine pennycress grows very well in soil that has too much zinc for other plants. The pennycress cleans out the zinc and other dangerous metals, such as cadmium, from the soil.

not get enough zinc, they do not grow very tall, and the grain they produce is poor. Other signs that a lack of zinc is affecting a plant are pale areas on the leaves and stems. The leaves are also often smaller than usual. Even a small zinc deficiency can reduce the production of grain by a third. More severe zinc deficiencies might stop the crop from growing at all.

Treating the soil

Many areas lack zinc, but the worst affected places are Central Asia and the Middle East, where more than half the soil needs more of the metal.

Farmers with zinc-poor soil spray it with zinc sulfate ($ZnSO_4$). The zinc in this compound dissolves in the soil very slowly, so each treatment may last for years.

Zinc in the body

ZINC FACTS	
Foods rich in zinc	**mg of zinc/100 g**
Oysters	more than 7
Liver	6–8
Beef	4
Milk powder	4
Cheese	2–4
Shrimp	2
Eggs	1
Milk	0.4
Yogurt	0.4

The human body needs a constant supply of zinc to stay healthy. This essential mineral plays a vital role in many body processes. For example, zinc aids growth and development in children and protects the body from disease. Some people take zinc supplements to fight colds and coughs. However, there is no definite scientific evidence that this works.

Zinc also helps enzymes control many of the chemical reactions taking place in the body, and plays an important role in the brain and nerves.

Recommended daily intake

Zinc is known as a trace element, because the body needs only very small amounts to stay healthy. The recommended daily intake of zinc is 15 milligrams of zinc for men, 12 milligrams a day for women, and 11 milligrams for children. (One milligram is one-thousandth of a gram.) Very young children, pregnant women, and elderly people need more zinc than others.

Zinc is found in most foods. Shellfish, such as oysters, are especially high in zinc, as are meat, eggs, cheese, and pulses, such as peanuts and beans.

Doctors think that zinc might be important for memory. This student is being tested as part of a program investigating this. The test will check how well she remembers pictures and how the levels of zinc in her body affect this.

Food is the main source of zinc, and different foods contain different amounts of zinc. Sources include red meat (such as steak), poultry (such as chicken), liver, fish, shellfish, grains, and dairy products. There is a tiny amount of zinc in drinking water.

Zinc deficiency

Many people do not get enough zinc in their diets. Scientific studies have shown that nearly half of the world's population may suffer from not getting enough zinc. People who have a lack of zinc in their body suffer from several problems. Their sense of taste and smell stop working as well and they often get skin problems. Their hair may fall out and many people feel tired all the time. A lack of zinc means that people find it hard to fight off illnesses and might also find it harder to have children.

Most people at risk of these problems live in developing countries and in poor communities, where they cannot get hold of enough healthy food.

Too much zinc

Zinc is not poisonous but too much zinc in the diet may cause problems. High levels of zinc are linked to stomach problems and damage to the immune system, which fights disease. Too much zinc also stops the the body from absorbing the copper and iron it needs. Inhaling zinc oxide powder causes shivering, called zinc chills.

Periodic table

Everything in the universe is made from combinations of substances called elements. Elements are made of tiny particles called atoms, which are too small to see.

The character of an atom depends on how many even tinier particles called protons there are in its center, or nucleus. An element's atomic number is the same as the number of its protons.

Scientists have found around 116 different elements. About 90 elements occur naturally on Earth. The rest have been made in experiments.

All these elements are set out on a chart called the periodic table. This lists all the elements in order according to their atomic number.

The elements at the left of the table are metals. Those at the right are nonmetals. Between the metals and the nonmetals are the metalloids, which sometimes act like metals and sometimes like nonmetals.

- On the left of the table are the alkali metals. These have just one outer electron.

- Metals get more reactive as you go down a group. The most reactive nonmetals are at the top of the table.

- On the right of the periodic table are the noble gases. These elements have full outer shells.

- The number of electrons orbiting the nucleus increases down each group.

- Elements in the same group have the same number of electrons in their outer shells.

- The transition metals are in the middle of the table, between Groups II and III.

Group I

Group II

Transition metals

1 H Hydrogen 1								
3 Li Lithium 7	4 Be Beryllium 9							
11 Na Sodium 23	12 Mg Magnesium 24							
19 K Potassium 39	20 Ca Calcium 40	21 Sc Scandium 45	22 Ti Titanium 48	23 V Vanadium 51	24 Cr Chromium 52	25 Mn Manganese 55	26 Fe Iron 56	27 Co Cobalt 59
37 Rb Rubidium 85	38 Sr Strontium 88	39 Y Yttrium 89	40 Zr Zirconium 91	41 Nb Niobium 93	42 Mo Molybdenum 96	43 Tc Technetium (98)	44 Ru Ruthenium 101	45 Rh Rhodium 103
55 Cs Cesium 133	56 Ba Barium 137	71 Lu Lutetium 175	72 Hf Hafnium 179	73 Ta Tantalum 181	74 W Tungsten 184	75 Re Rhenium 186	76 Os Osmium 190	77 Ir Iridium 192
87 Fr Francium 223	88 Ra Radium 226	103 Lr Lawrencium (260)	104 Rf Rutherfordium (263)	105 Db Dubnium (268)	106 Sg Seaborgium (266)	107 Bh Bohrium (272)	108 Hs Hassium (277)	109 Mt Meitnerium (276)

Lanthanide elements

Actinide elements

57 La Lanthanum 39	58 Ce Cerium 140	59 Pr Praseodymium 141	60 Nd Neodymium 144	61 Pm Promethium (145)
89 Ac Actinium 227	90 Th Thorium 232	91 Pa Protactinium 231	92 U Uranium 238	93 Np Neptunium (237)

The horizontal rows are called periods. As you go across a period, the atomic number increases by one from each element to the next. The vertical columns are called groups. Elements get heavier as you go down a group. All the elements in a group have the same number of electrons in their outer shells. This means they react in similar ways.

The transition metals fall between Groups II and III. Their electron shells fill up in an unusual way. The lanthanide elements and the actinide elements are set apart from the main table to make it easier to read. All the lanthanide elements and the actinide elements are quite rare.

Zinc in the table

Zinc is a member of the transition metals. However, unlike most other transition metals all of a zinc atom's inner electron shells are full. Therefore, zinc's chemistry is more like members of Group II. Zinc is more reactive than most other metals. It reacts with all acids and it often replaces the metal elements in salt compounds.

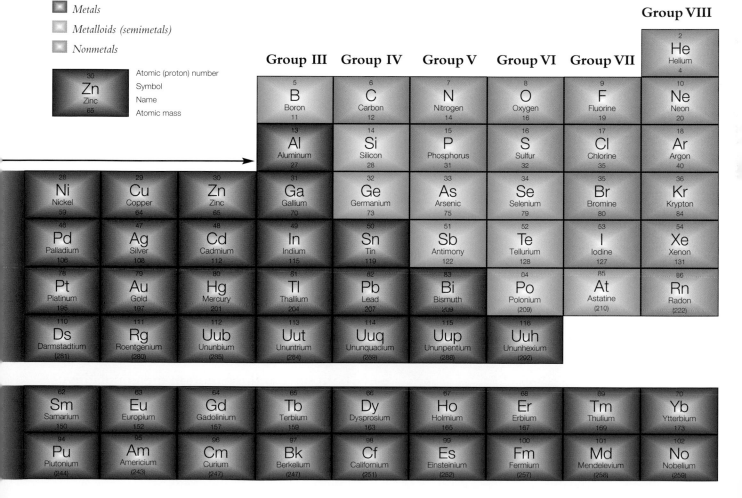

Chemical reactions

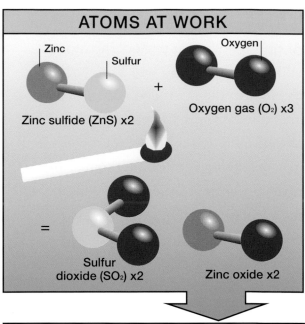

Zinc
Sulfur
Oxygen

Zinc sulfide (ZnS) x2
Oxygen gas (O₂) x3

=

Sulfur dioxide (SO₂) x2
Zinc oxide x2

Chemical reactions are going on around us all the time. Some reactions involve just two substances; others many more. But whenever a reaction takes place, at least one substance is changed.

In a chemical reaction, the number and type of atoms stay the same. But they join up in different combinations to form new molecules.

Solid zinc reacts with a solution of lead nitrate to make solid lead and a solution of zinc nitrate.

The reaction that takes place can be written like this:

$$2ZnS + 3O_2 \rightarrow 2ZnO + 2SO_2$$

This tells us that two molecules of zinc sulfide react with three molecules of oxygen to give two molecules of zinc oxide and two molecules of sulfur dioxide gas.

Writing an equation

Chemical reactions can be described by writing down the atoms before and after the reaction. The number of atoms before is the same as the number of atoms after. Chemists write the reaction as an equation. This shows what happens in the reaction.

When the numbers of each atom on both sides of the equation are equal, the equation is balanced. If the numbers are not equal, something is wrong. So the chemist adjusts the number of atoms involved until the equation balances.

Glossary

acid: An acid is a chemical that releases hydrogen ions easily during reactions.

atom: The smallest part of an element having all the properties of that element.

atomic mass number: The number of protons and neutrons in an atom.

atomic number: The number of protons in an atom.

bond: The attraction between two atoms, or ions, that holds them together.

compound: A substance made of two or more elements chemically joined together.

corrosion: The eating away of a material by reaction with other chemicals, often oxygen and moisture in the air.

crystal: A solid consisting of a repeating pattern of atoms, ions, or molecules.

electrode: A material through which an electrical current flows into, or out of, a liquid electrolyte.

electrolysis: The use of electricity to change a substance chemically.

electrolyte: A liquid that electricity can flow through.

electron: A tiny particle with a negative charge. Electrons are found inside atoms, where they move around the nucleus in layers called electron shells.

element: A substance that is made from only one type of atom. Zinc is one of the transition metals.

ion: An atom or a group of atoms that has lost or gained electrons to become electrically charged.

mineral: A compound or element as it is found in its natural form in Earth.

metal: An element on the left-hand side of the periodic table.

molecule: A unit that contains atoms held together by chemical bonds.

nucleus: The dense structure at the center of an atom. Protons and neutrons are found inside the nucleus of an atom.

neutron: A tiny particle with no electrical charge. Neutrons are found in the nucleus of almost every atom.

ore: A mineral or rock that contains enough of a particular substance to make it useful for mining.

periodic table: A chart of all the chemical elements laid out in order of their atomic number.

proton: A tiny particle with a positive charge. Protons are found in the nucleus.

reaction: A process in which two or more elements or compounds combine to produce new substances.

slurry: A watery mixture of solid powder.

solution: A liquid that has another substance dissolved in it.

transition metal: An element positioned in the middle of the periodic table. As well as having spaces in their outer electron shell, most transition metals also have spaces in the next outermost shell.

Index